Book of Joel—Bible Studies

Paul J. Bucknell

A Brief Study of The Future

Books by Paul J. Bucknell

Allowing the Bible to speak to our lives today!

Overcoming Anxiety: Finding Peace, Discovering God

Life in the Spirit! Experiencing the Fullness of Christ

The Lord Your Healer: Discover Him and Find His Healing Touch

Reaching Beyond Mediocrity: Being an Overcomer

The Life Core: Discovering the Heart of Great Training

The Godly Man: When God Touches a Man's Life

Redemption Through the Scriptures

Godly Beginnings for the Family

Principles and Practices of Biblical Parenting

Building a Great Marriage

Christian Premarital Counseling Manual for Counselors

Relational Discipleship: Cross Training

Running the Race: Overcoming Sexual Lusts

The Bible Teaching Commentary on Genesis

The Bible Teaching Commentary on Romans

Life Transformation: A Monthly Devotional on Romans 12:9-21

Book of Romans: Bible Studies

Book of Ephesians: Bible Studies

Book of Joel—Bible Studies: A Brief Study of the Future

Abiding in Christ: Walking with Jesus

Inductive Bible Studies in Titus

1 Peter Bible Study Questions: Living in a Fallen World.

Take Your Next Step into Ministry

Training Leaders for Ministry

Studies for Building Strong Marriages

Satan's Four Stations: The Destroyer is Destroyed

Study Questions for Jonah: Understanding the Heart of God

Check out these and other valuable resources like our digital online libraries at www.foundationsforfreedom.net

Book of Joel—Bible Studies

A Brief Study of the Future
Paul J. Bucknell

Book of Joel—Bible Studies: A Brief Study of the Future
Copyright ©2017 Paul J. Bucknell

Printed paperback:
ISBN-13: 978-1-61993-047-6

Also Digital e-book
ISBN-13: 978-1-61993-059-9

www.foundationsforfreedom.net
Pittsburgh, PA 15212 USA

The NASB version is used unless otherwise stated.
New American Standard Bible ©1960, 1995 used by permission, Lockman Foundation www.lockman.org.

All rights reserved. Limited production is acceptable without prior permission for home and educational use. For extensive reproduction contact the author at:
info@foundationsforfreedom.net

Dedication

Praise to God who from eternity controls the future, magnificently proclaims and displays in time His abounding grace and truth in our lives and to the nations.

Appreciation

God's insights are amazingly distributed throughout the Scriptures so that we can, bit by bit, grow in truth and excitement. Praise be to His Name!

I am also very appreciative of my daughter, Allison Bucknell-Herrera, who made time to edit this book while she was planning her wedding.

Table of Contents

Preface	11
Introduction of Joel	15
Study 1: The Book of Joel An Introduction	17
Study 2: The Book of Joel Introduction continued	19
Study 3: The Book of Joel Chapter 1:1-20	21
Study 4: The Book of Joel Chapter 2:1-11	25
Reflection 1: Joel 1:1-2:11 The Judgment We Deserve	31
Study 5: The Book of Joel Chapter 2:12-17	35
Study 6: The Book of Joel Chapter 2:18-27	41
Reflection 2: Joel 2:12-27 The Grace We Do Not Deserve	47
Study 7: The Book of Joel Chapter 2:28-32	53
Reflection 3: Joel 2:28-32 Marks of Abounding Grace	59
Study 8: The Book of Joel Chapter 3:1-21	67
Reflection 4: Joel 3:1-21 The End and the Beginning	73
Author Introduction	77

Preface

Purpose of Studying the Book of Joel

The Book of Joel not only supplies us a fantastic sampling of the Old Testament prophetic books but also provides insight into how to interpret prophetic books to cast light on the future (i.e., eschatology). Join us in this brief study; study a little, gain a lot!

My Interest in Joel

My particular interest in Joel was revived when preaching through the Book of Acts. A certain section of Joel (Joel 2:28-32) was so clearly interpreted in Acts 2 as a prediction for the Pentecost event. Did Joel really speak so clearly about that event? If so, would he not have also powerfully spoken of other significant end time events?

The Profit of Studying Joel

Readers will not be disappointed in this study of the Book of Joel. Let us consider this book as a prophetic primer. Although there are varying views on eschatology, many believers have only heard of one perspective, and, coupled with a common neglect of Old Testament study, have become confused on themes like judgment, salvation, mercy, and the end times. Joel provides just the right setting in which we can settle on a number of basic but critical interpretational (i.e., hermeneutical) factors from which we can then launch further investigations into other sources to grasp the important topic of the end of the world.

Understanding the Last Days

The topic of the last days is again surging with all the recent events in the Middle East. For example, the president has announced its decision to move the United States' embassy to Israel's capital of Jerusalem. This coming May 14, 2018, marks the 70th year of Israel, and some speculate that this will form a full generation signifying the prophetic calendar has again started to tick. At the same time, I challenge preachers and parents alike to be cautious of false prophets and teachers who bring up spurious teaching about the last times such as Harold Camping's past proclamation of the end of the world on May 21, 2011. Our people are asking numerous questions about the end of the world. Not all of the questions will be resolved with this study on Joel, but it does give us a small but powerful approach to using the Old Testament prophecies in modern times. Beyond this, there are other related theological teachings like the final judgment, calamities, and the doctrines of hell that are being strongly contested in our modern world.

Why not join us in this brief study of eight lessons?

Expectations for this Study of Joel

Before getting into this study of Joel, let me introduce the format we will use along with some of my own expectations.

The introduction is followed by a section-by-section study of the Book of Joel, eight studies in all. Our hope is that through the guided study questions and theological reflections you will be able to enjoy the Book of Joel, see how it is relevant to you and those around you, and gain special insight into the basic theology of the last days.

However, I realize that many people are very unsure about how to handle prophetic passages so I have included four Reflection chapters, positioned after the relevant studies, so one can more objectively compare his or her conclusions with an outside objective source.

Our understanding and confidence in handling prophetic passages will grow with our knowledge, discussions, and reading, but it is critical that our basic foundational framework of understanding prophetic passages is laid by careful bible study and conclusions. We should insist on integrity to the scriptures– "Where is this taught in the scriptures?" "How sure are you about the interpretation?" "Are there other possible interpretations?" "What makes you so confident that this is the right interpretation?"

Using Other Sources

Some might be disappointed with the lack of scholarly comments. Our "Reflection" sections should reduce that, but if you are so inclined to use commentaries, only let them be a supplement to your studies. Your richest studies occur when you personally explore the message of the book as it forces you to reflect on what the text says and means and what God is trying to say in His Word. If you know Hebrew, use it. We will minimize the use of specialized words to enable everyone to get involved in this study. Feel free to use theological terms in your responses and reflections.

We hope you do word studies to enrich your study. For those who don't know, a word study is one in which you trace the use of key words or phrases in a book or chapter. Online resources make this easy but be aware that sometimes different words are used in the original Hebrew for the same English word and that that can throw off one's conclusion.

Generally, we shun spending time on literary or 'higher' critical studies because of their biased and unbiblical assumptions. For example, they spend too much time on how many people have written a Bible book or how it was later edited (or even written!). We disagree with those assumptions and therefore refuse to engage in those discussions. We instead adopt Jesus' viewpoint, one that caused Him to memorize and live by God's Word. Jesus treated the Old Testament as fully trustworthy. As an example, note how Peter was convinced of Joel's authorship, "but this is what was spoken of through the prophet Joel" (Acts 2:16). God anointed Joel as a prophet and spoke through him; therefore, we ought to conclude that we should pay attention to the message of Joel rather than speculate whether Joel wrote this book.

We do, however, encourage a close examination of the original Hebrew manuscripts for differences (this kind of study is often called "lower criticism"). Some have the research tools and knowledge on how to do this. Only, be careful not to get sidetracked from the main study. While these side studies are often very helpful, they rarely relate to the main understanding.

Your Expectations for This Study

Surround your study with prayer. Allow each study in God's Word to form part of your personal spiritual adventure with Him. As you begin, first try to think through what you would like to learn from this study. This is somewhat difficult to do because you do not know what you will learn. Even still, though, specifically seek the Lord to teach you. Note any particular items or verses that He brings to your attention. The best studies occur when you consciously seek the Spirit to be your teacher. The briefness of this study helps the readers to focus on how prophetic events are introduced without getting distracted or overwhelmed.

Introduction of Joel

The time in which the Book of Joel was written is not clear. The first section, 1:1-2:27, clearly depicts the difficult situation of God's people, but we have no clue to what era it belongs. It was probably written after the capture of the northern kingdom because there is no mention of Samaria (i.e., Israel, the northern kingdom). This is, however, an argument from silence though Joel did not seem to have a provincial view but a larger perspective of his society at large.

Some suggest the Book of Joel was written after the exile (i.e., postexilic), but it seems to fit better with the tone of the books before the capture of Jerusalem and the southern kingdom.

The absence of historical points in this book is deliberate and is partially what gives it its extra thrust. The reader is cast into the future by deferring all time references to the distant future. Joel's prophetic eye, then, becomes a significant part of the book's design.

Verse Numbering

When discussing Joel, one needs to be careful about which verses one is discussing. The Hebrew Bible is laid out slightly different from the English translations. The differences begin at the end of chapter 2 as noted below. The verses are the same, but they are framed differently.

English Bible	Hebrew Bible
1:1-20	1:1-20
2:1-27	2:1-27
2:28-32	**3:1-5**
3:1-21	**4:1-21**

We will use the English version (NASB) for our study. Chapter and verse divisions are not part of the original manuscripts but were added later on. They are helpful and give us a little insight into the scribe's mind, but the verses should not influence one's interpretation.

The Reflection chapters hold commentary and perspectives of the preceding studies. Refer to these pages as needed. Many students rightly ask questions of the Old Testament's meaning, context, and connection to other prophetical books. I hope to encourage further confidence and reflection, that these chapters that would encourage others in their understanding and application of these passages.

Reflection #1: The Judgment We Deserve (Joel 1:1-2:11)

Reflection #2: The Grace We Do Not Deserve (Joel 2:12-27)

Reflection #3: Marks of God's Abounding Grace (Joel 2:28-32)

Reflection #4: The End and the Beginning (Joel 3:1-21)

I challenge teachers and preachers to seriously consider preaching through Joel to perfect their studies. The key prophetic passages in the last part of Joel are of great significance. Throughout your study, keep in mind what the book states regarding God's people as well as Israel as a nation.

Prophetic books differ in their focus. Many of them strive to bring repentance to the recipients. Joel would welcome that response but as it does not identify its recipients and their individual or corporate sins we are driven to think of the distant future when God will again actively work among His people.

Study 1: The Book of Joel
An Introduction

It is important to gain a big-picture idea of the Book of Joel before looking in detail at the individual verses so that we can better understand how individual verses and thoughts fit into the whole.

Gaining an Overview of Joel

1. Read the Book of Joel three times. Complete the following assignments as you do.

2. Make a chart with all references to time, dates, and events that are somehow linked to time. The lines do not indicate the number of references, so use less or more as needed.

Joel passage	Words describing time	Other insight

3. Identify any other references to persons, events, etc., that would help us know who Joel was writing to.

4. The book Amos follows Joel in the English Bible. Read two small sections of Amos, 2:1-3 and 2:4-5. Notice who is being addressed, how their sins are identified, and what judgment is articulated. How is this different from Joel 1?

5. Write a summary paragraph of your above discoveries.

6. Write out the most significant point of this study for you and pray through it.

Study 2: The Book of Joel Introduction continued

Before moving onto our main study, we need to better understand the development of the book. We do this by breaking the book into paragraphs so that we can see the flow of thought.

Discovering the Parts of Joel

1. Read the Book of Joel two times.

2. As you read, find and develop the major paragraph breaks. (Paragraphs break with new subject, author, or other shifts.)

3. Identify any struggles in your attempt to do this by writing a short paragraph describing the verses involved and the choices complicating the decision.

4. Provide brief section titles for each major portion.

5. Summarize what the Book of Joel is about and what God might be teaching through it.

6. Write out the most significant point of this study for you and pray it through.

Study 3: The Book of Joel
Chapter 1:1-20

Joel 1:1-20 Study Verses

1 The word of the LORD that came to Joel, the son of Pethuel. 2 Hear this, O elders, And listen, all inhabitants of the land. Has anything like this happened in your days Or in your fathers' days? 3 Tell your sons about it, And let your sons tell their sons, And their sons the next generation. 4 What the gnawing locust has left, the swarming locust has eaten; And what the swarming locust has left, the creeping locust has eaten; And what the creeping locust has left, the stripping locust has eaten. 5 Awake, drunkards, and weep; And wail, all you wine drinkers, On account of the sweet wine that is cut off from your mouth. 6 For a nation has invaded my land, Mighty and without number; Its teeth are the teeth of a lion, and it has the fangs of a lioness. 7 It has made my vine a waste, and my fig tree splinters. It has stripped them bare and cast them away; Their branches have become white.

8 Wail like a virgin girded with sackcloth For the bridegroom of her youth. 9 The grain offering and the libation are cut off From the house of the LORD. The priests mourn, The ministers of the LORD. 10 The field is ruined, The land mourns, For the grain is ruined, The new wine dries up, Fresh oil fails. 11 Be ashamed, O farmers, Wail, O vinedressers, For the wheat and the barley; Because the harvest of the field is destroyed. 12 The vine dries up, And the fig tree fails; The pomegranate, the palm also, and the apple tree, All the trees of the field dry up. Indeed, rejoicing dries up From the sons of men.

13 Gird yourselves with sackcloth, And lament, O priests; Wail, O ministers of the altar! Come, spend the night in sackcloth, O

ministers of my God, For the grain offering and the libation Are withheld from the house of your God. 14 Consecrate a fast, Proclaim a solemn assembly; Gather the elders And all the inhabitants of the land To the house of the LORD your God, And cry out to the LORD. 15 Alas for the day! For the day of the LORD is near, And it will come as destruction from the Almighty. 16 Has not food been cut off before our eyes, Gladness and joy from the house of our God? 17 The seeds shrivel under their clods; The storehouses are desolate, The barns are torn down, For the grain is dried up. 18 How the beasts groan! The herds of cattle wander aimlessly Because there is no pasture for them; Even the flocks of sheep suffer. 19 To Thee, O LORD, I cry; For fire has devoured the pastures of the wilderness, And the flame has burned up all the trees of the field. 20 Even the beasts of the field pant for you because the water brooks are dried up, and fire has devoured the pastures of the wilderness. (1:20 ESV)

Joel 1:1-20 Study Questions

1. Read Joel 1:1-20 and write down all the commands to the recipients. You might prefer to copy or print out a copy of the verses and highlight the verbs used and underline the commands instead.

2. Return to your original paragraph breaks and titles (c.f. Study #2). Review and adjust them as needed or make a new set based on these verses if needed. Explain why you might make any changes.

3. From Joel 1:1-3, what do you know about the author and recipients of Joel's message?

Study 3: The Book of Joel Chapter 1:1-20

4. Joel lists a number of judgments in 1:4-20. List (or highlight on a copy) each of them.

5. Which judgments have already come upon them and which are yet to come? Explain your answer.

6. How many times is 'wail' or similar words used in these verses?

7. Who does he address each time? How are the groups he addresses different? Do you see any progression?

8. Reflect on any scenes of wailing or devastation described here in chapter one that you have seen or heard about in your personal life. What stands out most to you?

9. Their sins are not mentioned. Do you think the evils that they face are related or unrelated to their sins? Please explain. Include 1:15 as part of your answer. (c.f. Amos 4:6-10, three deliberate links between their sins and His purpose in their return.)

10. None of their sins are listed here, making this chapter (and book) directed to societies everywhere. What devastations do you see around you? Do you think they just happen or are they related to the sins of your society?

11. Be sure to close this time with a prayer that includes grieving for the sins and evils you see and hear around you. Seek the Lord that He might help your people connect these forms of judgment with their sins so that they might repent.

12. Remember Jesus' caution from Luke 13:1-5 on our understanding of calamities. Read the passage carefully and answer the two following questions:

    - Did Jesus state that those calamities were due to their sins?

    - Did the absence of such calamities in other situations mean there were no ensuing sins to be judged?

13. Describe what you thought was the most significant point of this study and pray through it.

Study 4: The Book of Joel Chapter 2:1-11

Joel 2:1-11 Study Verses

1 Blow a trumpet in Zion, And sound an alarm on My holy mountain! Let all the inhabitants of the land tremble, For the day of the LORD is coming; Surely it is near, 2 A day of darkness and gloom, A day of clouds and thick darkness. As the dawn is spread over the mountains, So there is a great and mighty people; There has never been anything like it, Nor will there be again after it To the years of many generations. 3 A fire consumes before them, And behind them a flame burns. The land is like the garden of Eden before them, But a desolate wilderness behind them, And nothing at all escapes them. 4 Their appearance is like the appearance of horses; And like war horses, so they run. 5 With a noise as of chariots They leap on the tops of the mountains, Like the crackling of a flame of fire consuming the stubble, Like a mighty people arranged for battle. 6 Before them the people are in anguish; All faces turn pale. 7 They run like mighty men; They climb the wall like soldiers; And they each march in line, Nor do they deviate from their paths. 8 They do not crowd each other; They march everyone in his path. When they burst through the defenses, They do not break ranks. 9 They rush on the city, They run on the wall; They climb into the houses, They enter through the windows like a thief. 10 Before them the earth quakes, The heavens tremble, The sun and the moon grow dark, And the stars lose their brightness. 11 And the LORD utters His voice before His army; Surely His camp is very great, For strong is he who carries out His word. The day of the LORD is indeed great and very awesome, And who can endure it?

Joel 2:1-11 Study Questions

1. Read Joel 2:1-11 aloud with emphasis and write down all the commands to the recipients.

2. Has the Day of the Lord arrived or yet to come? See 1:15, 2:1. Defend your answer.

3. Find all the places the phrase "Day of the Lord" is used in Joel.

4. What is the problem identified in 1:13?

    In 1:16-20?

5. Are we supposed to think that droughts and famine are connected to God's dealings with us? Read 2 Chronicles 6:26-31. What did Solomon believe regarding the question of droughts and famines?

6. Have you ever experienced a fire, famine, or drought? Reflect on your experiences. How did they affect the smooth operation of a society as a whole?

7. When is an alarm usually sounded? Why is the alarm trumpet sounded in 2:1? Do you think our society needs an alarm sounded now? Why or why not?

8. Joel 2:2-11 forms a long description of the Day of the Lord. (1:15-20 formed a shorter but similar section). What danger is being described here in these verses? Write down at least four phrases from this section that would support your answer.

   •

   •

   •

   •

9. From what we have read and verse 2:11, would you say that the Day of the Lord generally describes judgment or is used as an end of a series of judgments resulting in complete desolation?

10. Sometimes we think God works with Israel as a nation different from other nations (including our own). Is this true or not? What difference does Peter state in 1 Peter 4:17?

11. Is the Day of the Lord also a New Testament concept? Can you think of where the term is used or alluded to? Check out these verses and see what similarities or differences you find:

    • 1 Corinthians 5:5

- 1 Thessalonians 5:2

- 2 Thessalonians 2:2

- 2 Peter 3:10

Summary

The day of the Lord, then, is the day God strikes judgment on any society. In a more specific way, the term "Day of the Lord" stands for the end of the world when God brings His full judgment to all mankind. Consider:

12. Are you ready for that day? Explain how your faith in Jesus can save you.

13. What part do you have in warning and preparing others for this great day?

14. Modern scoffers contest the message of those who preach on the subject of hell. They consider it an offensive four-letter offensive word. How does the concept of hell relate to judgment (i.e., The Day of the Lord)?

15. Does the New Testament give us an obligation or example to speak clearly of the judgment or hell? Can we speak of one rather than the other?

16. Write out the most significant point of this study for you and pray it through.

Reflection 1: Joel 1:1-2:11
The Judgment We Deserve

Judgment comes not because the Lord delights in judging His people but because it a self-induced consequence. Although specific sins are not articulated as in other prophetic books, the judgments and warnings of greater calamities are an assumed result of the evil in the lives of the audience.

If we find the signs of judgment, then we should understand that we have left our God, no matter how much good we think we are doing.

As we study Joel, we will follow the text's leading to focus on eschatological teachings, that is, teachings on the future.

Observations:

The study of Joel will not answer all our questions about the end times but will provide two things:

(1) Particular teaching relevant to our Christian lives, and

(2) Insight and confidence into particular details about the end times.

Study Points

1. Small judgments or crises point to a larger coming judgment known as the Day of the Lord or the final judgment. Only then will final justice come.

2. Societal troubles should provoke us to seriously search for links to sinful choices. (Check here for exceptions: Special training/purpose, Job, and pruning; John 15.)

3. Calamities, including war and natural disasters, should be seen as warnings for a greater coming judgment without repentance. These prejudgments act as warnings, calling us back to the Lord.

4. What will it take to bring our society to its knees and wail at the sin we have committed? We are too self-confident and proud. May we awaken earlier rather than later.

5. On the Day of the Lord, every person and society will come before the Lord for a thorough examination, and full justice will be meted out in the coming age.

6. Time hurries toward the Day of the Lord where judgment will be justly given. Mankind will at that time no longer be able to escape from the consequences of their disobedience and sin.

Reflection 1: Joel 1:1-2:11 The Judgment We Deserve

Counter observations

Our learning is sharpened when we compare what we are learning to what others around us believe. Here are a number of examples.

Biblical Study Points Versus (<=>) Worldly Counter Points

1. There is a final judgment <=> There is no God, no judgment

2. Troubles are linked to sin <=> Bad experiences happen at random

3. Calamities are linked to God's censuring <=> Calamities are random acts of mother nature (we are disturbing Gaia, the mother earth goddess, and upsetting balance)

4. The severity of problems is often related to our resistance <=> What I do is up to me. There is no such things as morals because all is relative.

5. The final judgment will be personal <=> There is no God and therefore no accountability for our actions. Fear of hell is absurd; religious priests use it to control people's behavior

6. There is an urgency to repentance <=> We should not get hung up on the apocalypse

Study 5: The Book of Joel Chapter 2:12-17

Joel 2:12-17 Study Verses

12 "Yet even now," declares the LORD, "Return to Me with all your heart, And with fasting, weeping, and mourning; 13 And rend your heart and not your garments. "Now return to the LORD your God, For He is gracious and compassionate, Slow to anger, abounding in lovingkindness, And relenting of evil. 14 Who knows whether He will not turn and relent, And leave a blessing behind Him, Even a grain offering and a libation For the LORD your God?

15 Blow a trumpet in Zion, Consecrate a fast, proclaim a solemn assembly, 16 Gather the people, sanctify the congregation, Assemble the elders, Gather the children and the nursing infants. Let the bridegroom come out of his room And the bride out of her bridal chamber. 17 Let the priests, the LORD'S ministers, Weep between the porch and the altar, And let them say, "Spare Thy people, O LORD, And do not make Thine inheritance a reproach, A byword among the nations. Why should they among the peoples say, 'Where is their God?'" (Joel 2:12-17)

Joel 2:12-17 Study Questions

1. Read Joel 2:12-27 aloud in your favorite translation.

2. What does 'yet even now" in 2:12 refer to?

3. Joel 2:12-26 is separated into two large chunks by the word "then" in verse 18. The Lord sets up a new cause and effect pattern. If one does ____, then ____ will happen. What is the cause, that is, the change of behavior that the Lord is seeking from them (12-17)? Write down at least five clauses that depict this change along with the verse numbers for each.

•

•

•

•

•

4. Joel 2:12 says, "Return to Me with all your heart." There are three elements found in this clause. Explain each.

   (1) "Return"

   (2) "to Me"

Study 5: The Book of Joel Chapter 2:12-17   37

   (3) "with all your heart"

5. How does the "fasting, weeping, and mourning" (also from 2:12) fit into the meaning of the above clause?

6. Joel 2:13 tells us how to return to the Lord: "Rend your heart and not your garments, Now return to the Lord your God." What does it mean to rend your heart? Feel free to look it up in a dictionary. Write a prayer that comes from such a heart.

7. Joel also elaborates why a return to the Lord is possible in verse 13. Explain. Define each key term or phrase in your own words.

8. The first part of 2:14 says, "Who knows whether he will not turn and relent." Can you remember another passage that illustrates this? Elaborate. Explain how 2 Samuel 24 is an example of this.

9. The last part of 2:14 is vague and has several possible interpretations. It could refer to leaving behind a little food during His fierce judgment (rather than Him consuming it), or more likely, that He would not destroy every last person but leave behind a remnant that would seek Him. Explain the last part of verse 14 the best you can, using an above interpretation or another.

10. Read 2:15. Where did we read of blowing a horn before?

    - In Numbers 10:3-8 instructions for blowing the horn are given. Why was a horn told to be blown?

    - To what might this horn refer to?

11. What were the people supposed to do to find possible reprieve at the sound of the trumpet? List at least five things from verses 15-17.

    (1)

    (2)

    (3)

    (4)

    (5)

Study 5: The Book of Joel Chapter 2:12-17

12. Use verses 15-17 to describe special marks of the "solemn assembly." What is the difference between this and an especially long prayer meeting?

13. The phrase "solemn assembly" has been used in recent days to call God's people to humbly gather to pray for an extended period, humbly seeking God's grace. Is this a good thing to do? What need might there be for someone to call for this in your region today?

14. Verse 16 says to "sanctify the congregation." What might it mean back then (also refer to Nehemiah 8-9)? What might it mean for us today?

15. Describe the most significant point from this study for you and pray through it.

Study 6: The Book of Joel Chapter 2:18-27

This study continues on from Joel 2:12-17. Refer to that section as needed to gain the full context for some questions in this study.

Joel 2:18-27 Study Verses

"18 Then the LORD will be zealous for His land, And will have pity on His people. 19 And the LORD will answer and say to His people, "Behold, I am going to send you grain, new wine, and oil, and you will be satisfied *in full* with them; and I will never again make you a reproach among the nations.

20 "But I will remove the northern *army* far from you, And I will drive it into a parched and desolate land, And its vanguard into the eastern sea, And its rear guard into the western sea. And its stench will arise and its foul smell will come up, For it has done great things." 21 Do not fear, O land, rejoice and be glad, For the LORD has done great things. 22 Do not fear, beasts of the field, For the pastures of the wilderness have turned green, For the tree has borne its fruit, The fig tree and the vine have yielded in full.

23 So rejoice, O sons of Zion, And be glad in the LORD your God; For He has given you the early rain for *your* vindication. And He has poured down for you the rain, The early and latter rain as before. 24 And the threshing floors will be full of grain, And the vats will overflow with the new wine and oil. 25 "Then I will make up to you for the years That the swarming locust has eaten, The creeping locust, the stripping locust, and the gnawing locust, My great army which I sent among you. 26 "And you shall have plenty to eat and be satisfied, And praise the name of the LORD your God, Who has dealt wondrously with you; Then My people will never be put to shame. 27 "Thus you will

know that I am in the midst of Israel, And that I am the LORD your God And there is no other; And My people will never be put to shame" (Joel 2:18-27).

Joel 2:18-27 Study Questions

1. Joel 2:18-27 forms the second large part of this section. How is Joel 2:18-27 different from the former part (2:12-17)? State a few general differences.

-

-

2. The significant word for this section is "then" in verse 2:18. What is being contrasted in this verse?

3. How are God's pity and care for Israel being contrasted in 2:12-17? (This answer might be similar to a prior one.)

4. The Hebrew word for zealous (*qana*) in 2:18 is often translated jealous or envy. What does this word mean? Write a translation that uses words that you often use.

5. What does the Lord say that He will now do for them in verse 19?

Study 6: The Book of Joel Chapter 2:18-27   43

6. What about verse 20? What will the Lord do for His people?

7. From your study of scriptures, what were the names of Israel's formidable foes to the north? For a complete study, refer to Jeremiah 13:20, Ezekiel 48:1, Zephaniah 2:13, and Daniel 11:40, or do a Bible search for "north."

8. Who is being addressed in verses 21 and 22? What are they being told?

9. Who is being addressed in verse 23? What are they being told to do? Why?

10. "Zion" is used 163 times throughout the scriptures (only 7 in the NT). What does it mean or refer to? See Psalm 48:1-2, 51:18.

11. Do you think "sons of Zion" (2:23) refers to the Jews in a certain place or all the Jews? Explain.

12. Joel continues to speak about the favorable effect of the climate upon their land and therefore the lives of the Israelites from 23 to 26. Would this be something new? Reflect upon the words "as before" in verse 23.

13. From what you have read so far in Joel (or elsewhere in the Bible), do you think the weather just happened to change or was it because of God's intervention? Explain.

14. What are the key words in verse 25? What is so significant about them?

15. Who was responsible for the locust invasion? Does the Lord seem reluctant to let us know that? Why are God's people so reluctant to acknowledge this today?

16. God's blessings are often associated with the bounty that our bodies need to have good physical lives. What words in verse 26 indicate this bounty?

17. What response should we see in their lives (2:26)? Is this true with us too?

18. What might the phrase "will never be put to shame" mean at the end of verse 26?

19. Verse 27 reveals a number of proper responses from people in right relationship with Him. List all the proper responses you can find in verse 2:27.

Study 6: The Book of Joel Chapter 2:18-27

-

-

-

20. What keeps God's people from being put to shame (2:27)?

21. Some people suggest that the God of the OT is different from the God of the NT. How do the two parts of this longer section show that God in the OT has both wrath and grace?

22. Why is it that many people do not see the link between climate change and the Lord's blessing or chastisement?

23. The Lord wants us to rejoice in Him always (Phil 4:4)? Gauge your "joy in the Lord level" through the past week (1 being low and 10 being high).

- Do you think that if we are not able to delight in Him that something is wrong? Explain your answer.

24. Can you accept God's chastisement of His people? For yourself, if necessary? Is it more merciful to allow a person to proceed into eternal judgment or to warn him?

- Is it necessary, then, for parents to also chastise their children? What is the difference between punishment and chastisement, if any?

25. Describe the most significant point from this study for you and pray through it.

Reflection 2: Joel 2:12-27
The Grace We Do Not Deserve

Although a humbling judgment is mentioned here, it is done in such a way that we can see the prophetic word sprinkled with words of grace.

> "Yet even now," declares the LORD, "Return to Me with all your heart, And with fasting, weeping, and mourning; 13 And rend your heart and not your garments. "Now return to the LORD your God, For He is gracious and compassionate, Slow to anger, abounding in lovingkindness, And relenting of evil. 14 Who knows whether He will not turn and relent, And leave a blessing behind Him, Even a grain offering and a libation For the LORD your God? 15 Blow a trumpet in Zion, Consecrate a fast, proclaim a solemn assembly... (Joel 2:12-15).

The Lord beckoned them to return to Him "now" (12). As long as the earth endures, God's promises of mercy continue to be proclaimed, exhorting all to come to Him.

God's people are presented with the promise of forgiveness and restoration if they would only return to Him. They are to come humbly, confessing their sins. They are to gather everyone around and repent before Him. This is the time for a solemn assembly that brings with it the hope of gaining God's forgiveness and mercy.

With their repentance, they have every hope that God will restore them to Him and the land's fruitfulness. In the case of Joel, they need not fear (2:21) but rejoice (2:23) in the abundance that the Lord will bring.

Above all, God wants to make His grace known in such a way that He alone will be magnified in their midst with the hope that others, those who do not belong to Him, will recognize His grace and come to Him (2:27).

Meaning of Joel 2:14

> NASB 14 Who knows whether He will not turn and relent, and leave a blessing behind Him, even a grain offering and a libation For the LORD your God?

> NIV 14 Who knows? He may turn and have pity and leave behind a blessing--grain offerings and drink offerings for the LORD your God.

The phrase "leave a blessing behind" in verse 14 is a bit unclear. Certainly, it hints at the possibility of finding relief in God's grace in times of judgment. Two possibilities come to mind, and the later is preferred.

(1) What constitutes that grace is a bit unclear. Remember when Manoah, Samson's father, offered up a sacrifice and the Lord accepted the sacrifice? The whole thing is consumed in a fire unto the Lord (Judges 13:20). The blessing, in this case, would mean that the Lord left part of the offering behind for them to eat. Or it could be symbolic in that God's wrath would not consume everything but would leave behind a remnant along with some crops. Or, in other words, God would give grace at the time of judgment. David found this in 2 Samuel 24 after he counted the men and found grace during God's judgment.

(2) More unclear, perhaps, is the second part of the verse. It could refer to two things.

1. God would not consume everything but leave a bit behind.
2. God would keep some of His people alive so that they could offer up sacrifices to please Him.

Meaning of 2:15 Blow a trumpet

Where is the trumpet blown? Instructions for blowing the horn are given in Numbers 10:3-8. Why was it instructed that a horn be blown? It seems that a blown horn gathers the people around the Lord to seek His grace from the enemy. In this case, God Himself seems to be both the chief adversary as well as the interceder.

The Hebrew word for "then" (waw) could also be translated as "and." The context largely brings out this contrast, justifying the "then."

God is jealous of His people (2:18-19)

In Joel 2:18-19, we observe a transition from the third person to the first ("he," "she" to "me" or "my" or "I"). Joel first stated things that Lord Yahweh would do, but then, the Lord Himself began to speak. It is as if Joel was recording what He saw the Lord would do and then all of a sudden began hearing the Lord speak on behalf of His people. "And I will..." (end of 19) and "But I will..." (beginning of 20).

Two significant changes occur when the Lord's mercy comes with the Lord's change of treatment toward His people. God states that they will find great agricultural blessings. Joel 2:19 does mention the word oil, and this is in reference to olive oil rather than crude oil.

Judgment from the north

The mention of a "northern army" is one of the few indicators of the Book of Joel's time era, except that the term is so general and oft-used that this indicator does not specifically indicate the time of writing with any confidence, though does exclude certain enemies like Moab or Egypt. Many countries were included in the north, including Syria, Assyria, and Babylon. Some countries were located in Israel's northeast, such as Persia, but because of the roads circling about the desert region, they were still considered to be from the north.

God's care for His people

This section reveals much about God's dealings with His wayward people. The Lord is not interested in a simple and clean judgment of His people for He loves them too much and has greater goals in restoring them. We should realize, however, that God will sometimes withhold His blessing so that His people return to Him with the right heart, and then He will "repay" or "make up to" them His blessings (2:25).

Many Christians, unfortunately, have a difficult time grasping evil, whether it be chastisement that affects God's people or judgment for the world. God is not the author of this evil, but surely He does not disassociate His Name from the plague that comes upon His people, such as locusts devouring the land ("My great army which I sent among you" 2:25). Along with such crop devastation, many Israelites probably also died from hunger.

The balancing point here is God's grace. With the same people—though perhaps another generation—God will return and bring His blessing. The timing has everything to do with when the people who receive this message humble themselves, just as the first part of this section describes (2:12-17).

What typically happens is that God's people are too arrogant to learn from the warnings of the prophets and smaller forms of chastisement. God is not intent on punishing His people for punishment's sake (like His judgment), but conducts miniature judgments upon his children to serve as a retooling process. He is making them suitable because He cares for them. My daughter could have bought a new chair for her room, but instead, she took this old broken down chair and rebuilt the whole seat, first by "destroying" it. It took many hours for her to take it apart and repair it, but she intended to to repurpose it for use. In the same way, God is building up His people. He wants to bring His favor to His people and display His glory, but at times He has to deal harshly with them before rewarding them that they do not continue on in their evil deeds and live apart from being conscious of God's care for them.

God works with His people in such a way that they are restored, built up, and never need to go through that horrific process again (cf., Rev. 19-21).

Before we can understand prophecy, we must understand God's person and purpose. The first chapters of Joel are given to affirm God's true person and character which becomes the launchpad into predicting distant events and scenes, all of which relate to God's unfailing love for His people.

Study 7: The Book of Joel Chapter 2:28-32

Please note that Joel 2:28-32 is differently organized in the Hebrew Bible as 3:1-5. The text does not change but only its reference.

Joel 2:28-32 Study Verses

"28 And it will come about after this that I will pour out My Spirit on all mankind; And your sons and daughters will prophesy, Your old men will dream dreams, Your young men will see visions. 29 And even on the male and female servants I will pour out My Spirit in those days. 30 And I will display wonders in the sky and on the earth, blood, fire, and columns of smoke. 31 The sun will be turned into darkness, and the moon into blood, before the great and awesome day of the LORD comes. 32 And it will come about that whoever calls on the name of the LORD Will be delivered" (Joel 2:28-32).

Joel 2:28-32 Study Questions

1. Who is the subject of Joel 2:28-32? How many times is the phrase "I will" used here?

2. In each case, fill in the blanks with the verse number and the verb along with the simple object.

- Verse 2:_____ "I will _____"

- Verse 2:_____ "I will _____"

- Verse 2:_____ "I will _____"

3. Joel 2:18 marks, perhaps, the biggest surprise in the Book of Joel. For review, quickly scan Joel 2:1-17 and contrast it with 2:18-27. Summarize the big change that 2:18 marks.

4. What might the "after this" in Joel 2:28 refer to? Do you think it leaps ahead to a time different from 2:18-27? Explain.

5. Describe to the best of your ability what "pour out My Spirit" might refer to (2:28)? Would it be a good thing?

6. Compare the blessings in 2:18-27 with those in 2:28-29. Would you say they are the same or different? How so?

7. Who are the recipients of the blessings in 2:18-27? What about in 2:28-29? What is so surprising about the latter?

8. Describe what the Lord will display (i.e., the third "I will") in 2:30-31.

Study 7: The Book of Joel Chapter 2:28-32

9. When will these signs occur (2:31)? Can we detect any prophetic sequence of events here? Explain.

10. Joel 2:32 provides a strong promise for the time just preceding the climactic day of the Lord (or the early part of it). What is this promise? Who will escape?

11. What might the phrase "calls on the name of the Lord" mean? Think of a time you or another might have called out someone's name.

12. The day of the Lord in 2:30-32 seems to be of the same type as the one described earlier in 2:1-11 but with a call to return to Him at the end (2:12-17). Even some of the same descriptions are used (sun and moon grow dark). What difference would you say there is between them, if any?

13. Peter quotes this passage in Acts 2:17-21. He unabashedly claims that what happened on Pentecost is what was prophesied in Joel 2:28-32. What similarities or fulfillment of Joel did Peter see? Explain each term below from a New Testament perspective.

- Pour out the Spirit

- On all mankind

- They shall prophesy (hint: speak in foreign languages)

- Sun and moon made dark (hint: think of the midday darkness at the crucifixion)

- Promise of rescue

14. Peter is convinced that what was said in Joel was fulfilled at Pentecost after Christ's resurrection. Are you convinced? Or are these prophetic verses referring yet to a still distant event in the future?

15. Are you a believer? In what sense has this promise impacted your life? Please personally respond to the questions below.

- Are you a Jew or from another race?

- Is the Spirit of God now at work in your life?

- Did God's judgment fall on Christ and as a result bring hope to you?

- Did you call upon the Lord to save you? When? Describe the circumstances.

16. Describe the most significant point from this study for you and pray through it.

Reflection 3: Joel 2:28-32
Marks of Abounding Grace

It appears that the section in 2:28-32 (Hebrew Bible 3:1-5) is used to highlight an example of what happens when God's people humble themselves. The two disciples speaking of the "hidden" resurrected Christ spoke, "Are you the only one visiting Jerusalem and unaware of the things which have happened here in these days?" (Luke 24:18). They continued sharing how the people had their hope in the mighty prophet, Jesus Christ.

Is it possible that the grieving of God's people became the key leading to the renewal that God was looking for and had planned for in Pentecost? This sadness prevailed over Israel during Acts 1 up to the proclamation in Acts 2 where the people were exhorted to see their sin. In Acts 2:37, we read, "They were pierced to the heart." This allowed for more grace and wonders to be released.

Most interesting is the way that Peter quotes and uses that passage to describe what had happened that day with the pouring out of the Spirit and the signs associated with Christ's death.

> 28 "And it will come about after this That I will pour out My Spirit on all mankind; And your sons and daughters will prophesy, Your old men will dream dreams, Your young men will see visions. 29 "And even on the male and female servants I will pour out My Spirit in those days. 30 "And I will display wonders in the sky and on the earth, Blood, fire, and columns of smoke. 31 "The sun will be turned into darkness, And the moon into blood, Before the great and awesome day of the LORD comes. 32 "And it will come about that whoever calls on the name of the LORD Will be delivered" (Joel 2:28-32).

I have discussed the relevance of this message elsewhere (Acts 2:14-40)[1], but it suffices to say here that Joel is prophesying of God's awakened grace and pouring out of the Spirit of God on His people, signs signifying the establishment of the New Covenant and the church. Note the marks of the New Covenant are of the same type but are greater than those of the Old Covenant. but are greater than those of the Old Covenant.

(1) God's Spirit poured out indicates a great amount being given in contrast to just a little having been given. This "poured out" idea is exemplified by Saul's anointing. At times, the Holy Spirit would come in His fullness upon him with the result that everyone would acknowledge Saul as a prophet. "Therefore it became a proverb: 'Is Saul also among the prophets?'" (1 Samuel 10:11).

In the case of Pentecost, we see a similar outpouring of the Holy Spirit.

> "And when the day of Pentecost had come, they were all together in one place. And suddenly there came from heaven a noise like a violent, rushing wind, and it filled the whole house where they were sitting. And there appeared to them tongues as of fire distributing themselves, and they rested on each one of them. And they were all filled with the Holy Spirit and began to speak with other tongues, as the Spirit was giving them utterance" (Acts 2:1-4).

There were some who used their limited experiences to interpret what they were seeing. They had no way to understand the pouring out of the Spirit and so said that they were drunk. This is precisely where Peter steps in and clarifies that this is the pouring out of the Spirit as was prophesied in Joel (Acts 2:14-16 and on).

(2) The Spirit of God was given to all mankind and not just Jews. This is a remarkable prophecy, especially when you keep in mind the

---

[1] http://www.foundationsforfreedom.net/References/NT/Acts/Acts_02_Pentecost/Acts_02_14-21_Be-Saved.html

Reflection 3: Joel 2:28-32 Marks of Abounding Grace

emphasis in Acts 2 regarding people being from all over the world present at the feast at that time. The nations were, one by one, remarkably listed.

> "Now there were Jews living in Jerusalem, devout men, from every nation under heaven. And when this sound occurred, the multitude came together, and were bewildered, because they were each one hearing them speak in his own language. And they were amazed and marveled, saying, "Why, are not all these who are speaking Galileans? And how is it that we each hear *them* in our own language to which we were born? Parthians and Medes and Elamites, and residents of Mesopotamia, Judea and Cappadocia, Pontus and Asia, Phrygia and Pamphylia, Egypt and the districts of Libya around Cyrene, and visitors from Rome, both Jews and proselytes, Cretans and Arabs--we hear them in our *own* tongues speaking of the mighty deeds of God" (Acts 2:5-11).

Note the emphasis here: people from every nation under heaven speaking in his own language—the list identifies nations from around the world, including far-reaching Parthians and Medes (Iran) and northern Africans (Libya around Cyrene) as well as modern-day Turkey where Paul the Apostle went on some of his journeys, i.e., Asia.

(3) God would be working in all the believers, no matter which sex, age, or status. "And it will come about after this That I will pour out My Spirit on all mankind; And your sons and daughters will prophesy, Your old men will dream dreams, Your young men will see visions. "And even on the male and female servants I will pour out My Spirit in those days" (Acts 2:28-29). This should be contrasted to the few that served in the court of the Old Testament temple, but even they were not allowed to enter the Holy of Holies.

There is no evidence of women speaking in these various languages, but it happened! In Acts 1:14 says, "These all with one mind were continually devoting themselves to prayer, along with the women, and Mary the mother of Jesus, and with His brothers." Later the scripture in Acts 2:1 says they were together in one place when the flame of fire rested on each person's head. Acts 2:3 emphasizes this and therefore includes the women as part of the group. This later would influence the church's structure on how women could equally worship God where the men were (different from the temple courts). These might not be significant prophesies for us, but they were important back then. In terms of future repeated fulfillment, this aspect of the prophecy might be hard to repeat because of the changes in our society today. We no longer would be surprised to see the Spirit of God move on slaves, women (1 Cor 14:34), and seniors.

(4) Changes in heaven would appear. Great changes occurred on that Pentecost Day, but we should also remember the event of the darkened heavens during the middle of the day Jesus died. This was no mere eclipse, for the darkness reigned for three hours. Even solar eclipses do not bring total darkness for anywhere near that length of time. It is true that this sign occurred fifty days prior to the day of Pentecost, but we have to recognize Peter saw it fulfilled, linking the prior event of the cross and its miracles with the Pentecost, even as the Passover, Leavened Bread, First fruits (Leviticus 23), and Pentecost feasts are integrally related by their timing (e.g., Pentecost being 50 days after the crucifixion).

There was no recording of any events in the heavens on the day of Pentecost. So there are only a few limited interpretations possible.

A) Peter was referring to the heavens turning dark during the crucifixion.

B) Although Peter quoted the whole text, he was referring only to part of it. This is not likely. He could have quoted the applicable text if only part of it made sense.

C) Peter was referring to the upcoming judgment that had not yet happened but soon would. This would be the judgment on

Reflection 3: Joel 2:28-32 Marks of Abounding Grace

Jerusalem in 70 A.D. This is possible. The key question, if it can be determined, is whether the sign was a confirming sign (which would require the timing to be closer) or as a trigger for the coming judgment.

Overall, along with the next point, it seems that simply connecting the earth's darkness (which never happened again) at Jesus' crucifixion as the key sign of God's judgment on Jerusalem in Christ.

The darkening of the earth and moon are often used figuratively to depict the defeat of a nation, such as in Joel 2:10. The destruction of Jerusalem in 70 A.D. would fully fulfill this prophecy. The rejection of Jesus is linked to the destruction of Jerusalem that Jesus referred to several times during His life. And yet, it makes more sense for the preceding darkness—50 days prior—which all were witnesses to, as a sign of implementing the New Covenant.

(5) Amazing happenings occurred on earth at that time.

Besides the spiritual impartation and the prophecies of men and women, we would see displays in the skies and on the earth.

> "And I will display wonders in the sky and on the earth, blood, fire, and columns of smoke. 31 The sun will be turned into darkness, and the moon into blood, before the great and awesome day of the LORD comes" (Joel 2:30-31).

What could all this mean? We are tempted to combine the previous point with this one. The separation of the events in the sky and earth are even spoken of in verse 30. Of most importance is that God is doing the displaying and broadcasting to all the networks.

The New Testament gospels clearly record several significant events that occurred during Jesus' death and resurrection. They would be called wonders, whether it be the tearing of the curtain, the great earthquake, or the resurrection of many dead people. This is combined with the sky turning dark from noon to 3 pm. All were amazed at such events so that even the centurion affirmed Christ's true identity as the Son of God.

> "Now the centurion, and those who were with him keeping guard over Jesus, when they saw the earthquake and the things that were happening, became very frightened and said, 'Truly this was the Son of God!'" (Matthew 27:54)

(6) Salvation would be offered to all who would believe.

The very last words of Joel 2:32 were not included in Peter's speech, namely,

> "For on Mount Zion and in Jerusalem there will be those who escape, as the LORD has said, even among the survivors whom the LORD calls."

Reflection upon this would be profitable. Is it merely that someone edited Peter's remarks, or that Peter himself shortened the verses or that the later words here stated have to do with another time, such as what Jesus predicts in 70 A.D.? And though 5,000 were saved that day, many more stubbornly refused to believe.

Perhaps, Peter picks up on this calling aspect found in Joel 2:32 in verse 39, "For the promise is for you and your children, and for all who are far off, as many as the Lord our God shall call to Himself" (Acts 2:39).

Summary

Jesus' death had brought a certain amount of grief to many Jews in Acts 2 and permitted God to release an outpouring of His saving grace. Follow the murder of the Messiah came mourning over Jerusalem, and God followed through by releasing an abundant portion of His grace verified by the signs and ongoing awakened people of God.

It cannot be verified that these words in 2:28-32 were a complete fulfillment of this prophecy of Joel in such a way to satisfy them to have no more future reference, but surely, like Peter, we are to believe the Pentecost events were an outgrowth of this prophecy and can be content not to keep looking for future fulfillment. It would probably be wise just to be at peace that this fulfillment was found on Christ's death on the cross, an event that the Lord would certainly want us to focus on.

Application

For us, hope is always around the corner if we would but grieve, mourn, and vigorously call out to our God. God would indeed break forth in abounding grace. Oh, why do we wait for tragedies to occur before solemn times happen? City solemn assemblies truly have their place in calling us to humble our hearts to keep a spiritual alertness about ourselves and tragedy away but also provide a format to seek a greater outpouring of God's Almighty grace, something we so desperately need!

Study 8: The Book of Joel Chapter 3:1-21

This third chapter takes us to view the scenes at the end of the world, far from what Joel saw around Israel upon writing this.

Joel 3:1-2 Study Verses and Questions

3:1 "For behold, in those days and at that time, when I restore the fortunes of Judah and Jerusalem, 2 I will gather all the nations, and bring them down to the valley of Jehoshaphat. Then I will enter into judgment with them there on behalf of My people and My inheritance, Israel, whom they have scattered among the nations; and they have divided up My land" (Joel 3:1-2).

1. Describe several things that are predicted in verses 3:1-2?

2. How do those prophesies work together, that is, how is the judgment of the nations related to the restoration of Israel?

3. When is the restoration supposed to take place (3:1)? How are we to understand when it will take place?

Joel 3:3-8 Study Verses and Questions

3 "They have also cast lots for My people, Traded a boy for a harlot, And sold a girl for wine that they may drink. 4

"Moreover, what are you to Me, O Tyre, Sidon, and all the regions of Philistia? Are you rendering Me a recompense? But if you do recompense Me, swiftly and speedily I will return your recompense on your head. 5 "Since you have taken My silver and My gold, brought My precious treasures to your temples, 6 and sold the sons of Judah and Jerusalem to the Greeks in order to remove them far from their territory, 7 behold, I am going to arouse them from the place where you have sold them, and return your recompense on your head. 8 "Also I will sell your sons and your daughters into the hand of the sons of Judah, and they will sell them to the Sabeans, to a distant nation," for the LORD has spoken.

4. What are a few things that the Lord picks out that the nations have done against His people in verses 3:3-6?

5. What will be the result of those and other offenses against God's people (3:7-8)?

Joel 3:9-16 Study Verses and Questions

9 Proclaim this among the nations: Prepare a war; rouse the mighty men! Let all the soldiers draw near, let them come up! 10 Beat your plowshares into swords, And your pruning hooks into spears; Let the weak say, "I am a mighty man." 11 Hasten and come, all you surrounding nations, And gather yourselves there. Bring down, O LORD, Thy mighty ones. 12 Let the nations be aroused And come up to the valley of Jehoshaphat, For there I will sit to judge All the surrounding nations. 13 Put in the sickle, for the harvest is ripe. Come, tread, for the wine press is full; The vats overflow, for their wickedness is great. 14 Multitudes, multitudes in the valley of decision! For the day of the LORD is near in the valley of decision. 15 The sun and

Study 8: The Book of Joel Chapter 3:1-21　　　　　　　　　　69

moon grow dark, And the stars lose their brightness. 16 And the LORD roars from Zion And utters His voice from Jerusalem, And the heavens and the earth tremble. But the LORD is a refuge for His people And a stronghold to the sons of Israel.

6. What commands does the Lord give the nations in verses 9-11?

7. How does this section, including the last line of verse 11 to verse 14, differ from the former verses in 9-11? Who is speaking to whom?

8. Use your own words to summarize the picture the scriptures are giving to us in verses 9-14. Make sure you identify the various groups/individuals involved.

9. What is the Day of the Lord called here in verse 14?

10. Out of the 26 times the phrase, "The Day of the Lord" is used in the Bible, how many are used in Joel? Find them all.

11. What other things are part of the Day of the Lord as recorded in verses 15-16?

12. Do God's people need to be scared as the nations surround them (16)? Why?

Joel 3:17-21 Study Verses and Questions

> 17 Then you will know that I am the LORD your God, Dwelling in Zion My holy mountain. So Jerusalem will be holy, And strangers will pass through it no more. 18 And it will come about in that day That the mountains will drip with sweet wine, And the hills will flow with milk, And all the brooks of Judah will flow with water; And a spring will go out from the house of the LORD, To water the valley of Shittim. 19 Egypt will become a waste, And Edom will become a desolate wilderness, Because of the violence done to the sons of Judah, In whose land they have shed innocent blood. 20 But Judah will be inhabited forever, And Jerusalem for all generations. 21 And I will avenge their blood which I have not avenged, For the LORD dwells in Zion.

13. What are one of the results of the Day of the Lord as described in verse 17-18? List at least four wonderful developments for God's people.

-

-

-

-

Study 8: The Book of Joel Chapter 3:1-21

14. What two nations are used to represent all the nations in verse 19?

15. How does the Lord explain His severe judgment against the nations in verse 19?

16. What does the Lord promise to do in verse 20? How is the Lord's treatment of His people different from the way He treats the nations?

17. What reason does the Lord give for the different treatment of His people than the nations as seen in verse 21?

18. Briefly scan the whole Book of Joel. Who is God judging in chapter 1? How is the judgment in the last chapter so different? Why?

19. Are the people of God more holy than the nations? Is this the reason God treats them better?

20. Do you think the scene in chapter 3 is one taken from the end of the world? Summarize what is supposed to happen in the end.

21. Find at least three references to the final Judgment Day in the New Testament, including one spoken of by Jesus. Write down what each verse might have to say about this time. Does it match what Joel says?

-

-

-

22. Describe the most significant point from this study for you and pray through it.

Reflection 4: Joel 3:1-21
The End and the Beginning

Chapter 3:1 (Hebrew Bible 4:1) begins with significant words: "For behold, in those days and at that time, when I restore the fortunes of Judah and Jerusalem."

> 3:1 "For behold, in those days and at that time, when I restore the fortunes of Judah and Jerusalem, 2 I will gather all the nations, and bring them down to the valley of Jehoshaphat. Then I will enter into judgment with them there on behalf of My people and My inheritance, Israel, whom they have scattered among the nations; and they have divided up My land" (Joel 3:1-2).

The first thing we observe is chronological timing, which happens after the first prophecy that took place in Pentecost (33 A.D.). Furthermore, we understand that it would be something that happens after the desolation of Judah and Jerusalem in 70 A.D. Israel had to be further decimated before it could be restored.

It is possible that Judah and Jerusalem are referred to in a symbolic way. They could refer to God's people, even to those who had just come to the Lord, but this seems contrary to the statements in the previous verses, especially when we compare "all mankind" (2:28) with "I will gather the nations" (3:2) for judgment.

There are other pertinent arguments too. For example, as one continues reading chapter 3, there is a genuine focus on Judah as a Jewish people in contrast to God's people prophesied about at the end of chapter 2. In the same way, the prophet is speaking about real foreign nations: "Tyre, Sidon, and all the regions of Philistia" (3:4) are in contrast to those who are not God's people (i.e., spiritual Gentiles).

Assuming these things, we can then expect to see Israel brought back to herself from all the distant lands. This we saw, since on May, 1948, Israel was again declared as a nation, marking a tremendous movement of Jews back to their homeland along with a revival of the ancient Hebrew language.

In the midst of this prophecy is a call for the nations to gather around Israel as vultures. "Hasten and come, all you surround nations and gather yourself there... Let the nations be aroused and come up to the valley of Jehoshaphat" (Joel 3:11-12). Note how Revelation 19:19-21 uses this scene, seemingly as a basis for its own.

> "And I saw the beast and the kings of the earth and their armies, assembled to make war against Him who sat upon the horse, and against His army. 20 And the beast was seized, and with him the false prophet who performed the signs in his presence, by which he deceived those who had received the mark of the beast and those who worshiped his image; these two were thrown alive into the lake of fire which burns with brimstone. 21 And the rest were killed with the sword which came from the mouth of Him who sat upon the horse, and all the birds were filled with their flesh" (Rev. 19:19-21).

Although they would come to decimate Israel, God would use this to gather Israel's enemies as a place of judgment—the Valley of Jehoshaphat (3:12). Today, there remains a great amount of hostility toward Israel. For unseen reasons, surrounding nations want to gobble her up and remove not only Israel's sovereignty but her existence!

At the same time, we curiously do not see a repentant spirit in Israel. As a nation, she is wicked and evil, often displaying many secular tendencies. It seems, with our limited perspective, that God will bring this onslaught of judgment and use it to awaken the nation of Israel to its peril and sin. They will actually be able to see how their

Reflection 4: Joel 3:1-21 The End and the Beginning

sin is connected to their oncoming judgment (much like in Acts 2 at the killing of Jesus) but they will repent, and so, God will intervene and save her. At that point, the "strangers," or enemies, will no longer be able to pass through her (3:17).

Verses 3:20-21 again assert that God not only has a plan for the nations but one for Israel in particular.

> "But Judah will be inhabited forever, And Jerusalem for all generations. 21 And I will avenge their blood which I have not avenged, For the LORD dwells in Zion" (Joel 3:20-21).

She is the last nation that the Lord will call to Himself at the end of time (after the Gentiles harden themselves, according to Romans 11). God will awaken Israel and invite her to shine forth His grace in the last moments of history to join spiritual Israel (all of God's people across the earth) for the last great outreach for the lost and quest for holiness. The New Jerusalem is seen as the completion of the people of God from Israel as well as all the nations mentioned in Revelation 21.

Author Introduction

Rev. Paul J. Bucknell teaches Christian leadership seminars around the world and has authored more than twenty books on topics that include Christian life, discipleship, godly living, biblical studies, call to ministry, marriage, parenting, and anxiety. His commitment to the scriptures, blend of knowledge from different fields, along with his deep care for the training of God's people brings many special insights into the creation of this book. *The Bible Teaching Commentary* series seeks to make master teachers of God's Word, those who are relentlessly committed to understanding and teaching God's Word with the power and relevance God has intended.

Paul has been married for almost forty wonderful years. With eight children and five grandchildren, Paul and his wife Linda continually see God's blessings unfold in their lives.

For more on Paul and Linda and the BFF ministry, check online at: www.foundationsforfreedom.net

Printed in Great Britain
by Amazon